Deck
Safety
Manual

Deck

Safety

Manual

Bruce A. Barker

Deck Safety Manual

Publisher's Cataloging-in-Publication Data

Bruce A. Barker

Deck Safety Manual / Bruce A. Barker

Includes bibliographic references and index.

ISBN 13: 978-0-9848160-3-3

1. Housing- Standards --Popular works. 2. Building laws--Popular works. 3. Dwellings--Design and construction--Standards--Popular works. I Title.

Contents

Contents

List of Illustrations

5. Stairs

6. Handrails and Guardrails

7. Framing

8. Support Posts and Footings

Acknowledgements

Special thanks to:
The researchers at Virginia Tech University, Dr. Joe Loferski, and Dr. Frank Woeste, and Dr. Don Bender at Washington State University for their generous assistance. Their research has provided tested deck connection details and design information needed for additions to the model building codes. Their research has also provided a basis for better deck construction practices, and information about the importance of maintenance and inspection. We also acknowledge the assistance of Roger Robertson, Chesterfield County, Virginia Building Inspector (retired).

ILLUSTRATIONS

Bruce A. Barker, ACI
Dream Home Consultants, LLC.
Cary NC 27518

PHOTOGRAPHS

Alajajian, Lisa, ACI
    HomeQuest Consultants
    Milford MA 01757

Barker, Bruce, ACI
    Dream Home Consultants, LLC.
    Cary NC 27518

Cory, Shannon, ACI
    Rainbow Home Inspections
    Fayetteville GA 30214

Hankey, Roger, ACI
    Hankey & Brown Inspection Services
    Eden Prairie MN 55344

Robertson, Roger
    Building Inspector, Retired
    South Chesterfield VA 23803

Introduction

This book is not for everyone.

If you are thinking of building a deck,

this book is for you.

If you have a deck and have not had it inspected

at least once a year,

this book is for you.

People like outdoor living spaces. For many, this outdoor living space is a deck. People like to build things. For some, building a deck is a good way to get that outdoor living space.

Even if you are an indoor person who does not usually build things, there is a good chance that at some point you will consider adding a deck to your home. Before you consider building a deck, or even walking on one, you should be aware of the potential for deck disasters; make sure you, your family, and your friends are not victims of a deck disaster.

Tragically, deck disasters are known to occur at some of the most important times for a family, for example: birthdays, weddings and showers, graduations, and wakes.

> According to the Consumer Product Safety Commission (CSPC), an average of 120,989 people per year are injured, and 54 die because of the structural failure or collapse of a deck, porch, railing, or staircase. Many of those injured suffer traumatic injuries.

It is impossible to know with perfect accuracy the number of injuries that have gone unreported. Instances of serious injury and of fatalities are listed on the web pages of some law firms. Each year, there are also countless newspaper articles describing deck related failures. Experts at Virginia Tech estimate that there is at least one unreported failure each week.

Deck building standards and practices have changed dramatically since I began building homes in 1987. The standards and practices have changed even more in the last ten years.

Only a few years ago, deck building was a weekend job which allowed carpenters to make some extra money, or it was a do-it-yourself (DIY) project for cost-conscious homeowners. Few people had any appreciation for the forces that act on decks, or for the complexities involved in building a deck that would be safe, not only when it was built, but for its entire service life. Due to this lack of understanding, it is not surprising that deck disasters are common. If anything, it is surprising that deck disasters are not more common.

Ledger: A ledger is a horizontal support for deck and balcony floor joists that is attached to the house wall using bolts or lag screws.

Barker, *Everybody's Building Code*, 2015.

While the model building codes such as the 2000 (and later) *International Residential Code* (IRC) contained load requirements for deck components, they did not contain prescriptive methods whereby a contractor had guidance on how to construct a deck that met the IRC requirements. Virginia Tech and Washington State Universities conducted ledger connection tests for typical deck lumber species and created a deck ledger connection table that was first adopted by the 2003 Virginia Construction Code and later incorporated into the 2007 *IRC Supplement*.

Another result of this research was that the best deck building practices, as outlined in the *Design Code for Acceptance: Prescriptive Residential Wood Deck Construction Guide* (DCA6-12), incorporated the ledger connection and guardrail post connection data as early as 2007. As of this writing, DCA6-12 is the go-to document for how to build and inspect a deck. See Appendix II for a FREE link to this document.

> Note: while many articles use the term guardrails, the IRC uses the term guards.

The IRC changes slowly. Even the 2015 edition contains only some of the DCA6-12 best practices. Earlier IRC editions contain fewer best practices, and the model codes prior to 2006 have little to say about decks.

> Best practice recommendations and the building code requirements are not the same thing.

Adoption of the IRC by local code enforcement departments is slow. It usually takes at least a couple of years, often longer, for local code enforcement departments to adopt the new IRC editions. In addition, some local departments have the option to modify the IRC requirements. Thus, some progressive code enforcement departments have adopted some or all of the best practices in DCA6-12, while other departments have yet to adopt newer standards.

This book attempts to make a few important points about decks:

1) building and inspecting decks is more complicated than many people realize,

2) evaluating an existing deck is substantially more difficult than inspecting a new deck; the materials of an existing deck may have deteriorated, but the deterioration may not be apparent,

3) building and inspecting decks should not be a do-it-yourself (DIY) project for most people,

4) homeowners cannot rely on code enforcement officials to ensure that their deck conforms to best practices; code officials are generally limited by the code adopted in their jurisdiction,

5)   whether deck construction is DIY or by building professionals, the homeowner should always obtain permits, and have building inspections as required by the appropriate municipality.

Review codes before it's too late:

When building my deck, I constructed a little gabled structure on the back half where I could put the gas grill, and I sized it so that the grill could go up against the back railing. When I had the structure inspected, my inspector was kind enough to alert me to the fact that because I had flammable materials in the deck railing, I was going to have to move the grill forward 18 in., which then put me directly in the drop line of the gable above. Instead of getting wet, I would get drenched. The lesson here:

Before you add any structure to your deck, consult your local inspector---or you may end up all wet.   Miller, September 2012.

If deck building and deck inspecting is so complicated, what is the point of this book?

The point of this book is to alert you to some of the most important deck safety issues.

With this information, you can gather more detailed information about building a safe deck.

The information in this book will help you select qualified professionals who will help make sure that you, your family, and your friends are not victims of a deck disaster.

1

Why Deck Disasters Happen

Deck disasters, especially deck collapses, get good press coverage; however, it is difficult to obtain reliable information about how many injuries involving decks occur each year. Conservative estimates from the mid-2000s are in the 4,000 per year range, while other estimates from that period put the number closer to 35,000. Either way, there are a lot of injuries and deaths, most of which are preventable.

Part of the problem is that until about 2006 building codes had little to say about decks. The current model building code, the *2015 International Residential Code* (IRC), has much more to say about good deck building practices. It is, however, still silent about many important deck construction issues.

Lack of building code requirements and inconsistent enforcement of those requirements means that millions of decks may have significant problems that could result in injury. Problems are more likely in decks that are older than ten years. Reasons for these problems include weak building codes and enforcement, and also the fact that older decks are approaching, or are past the end of their service lives.

While this lack of code requirements and enforcement is disturbing, there is good news for those who want safe and well-built decks. Since 2001 research and testing at Virginia Tech by Dr. Frank Woeste and Dr. Joe Loferski, and work by the American Wood Council, have been used to make recommendations that have been adopted by the Virginia Building Code and the International Residential Code.

"Virginia is the leader in code development because folks like Woeste and Loferski care about the life safety issues that safeguard our buildings," said Roger Robertson, Chief of Inspections with the Chesterfield County (retired), Virginia, Department of Building Inspections.

One significant result of this work is the document *DCA6-12*. (See Appendix II for a link to the FREE download of *DCA6-12*, the *Prescriptive Residential Wood Deck Construction Guide Based on the 2012 International Residential Code*. Courtesy of the American Wood Council.)

Most deck disasters occur because of poor installation or maintenance in one or more of four essential deck components. These components are:

1) flashing,

2) ledger attachment,

3) stairs, and

4) handrails and guardrails.

Other deck components, such as support posts and footings, are important too, but these four components account for the vast majority of deck disasters.

1) FLASHING: Deck flashing keeps water from infiltrating behind the deck and into the house. Water can weaken the deck ledger attachment to the house so that the deck can pull away from the house and collapse. Water damage to the deck ledger attachment is a major factor in catastrophic deck failures. Water also damages other components inside the house and provides the moisture that mold needs to grow.

2) LEDGER ATTACHMENT: Most decks use the house as one of the structural supports, and deck ledger attachment to the house is essential to keeping the deck structure intact and safe. Until recently, deck builders were mainly concerned about downward forces acting on decks. Decks were attached using nails because, when correctly installed, they are good at resisting downward forces. **Recent university studies have shown that horizontal forces acting to pull the deck away are more important. Now, deck ledgers are attached using bolts, screws or other hardware that resist horizontal forces much more effectively than nails.**

3) STAIRS: Stairs are risky when located inside the house. Deck stairs are especially risky for additional reasons. Because deck stairs are exposed to the elements, they deteriorate faster than interior stairs. Because deck stairs are often improperly supported and are often poorly attached at the top landing, they can work loose from their supports and collapse.

4) HANDRAILS and GUARDRAILS: Handrails and guardrails are also risky systems. As with stairs, deck handrails and guardrails are exposed to the elements. Construction methods have also been called into question. Studies conducted at Virginia Tech have shown that many of the traditionally accepted guardrail attachment methods do not, and never have, resisted the code-mandated 200 pounds of horizontal force. In addition, normal wear and tear can lead to decreased performance of the fasteners that secure the guardrails and balusters to the deck. For example, balusters are required to resist 50 pounds of horizontal force. Deterioration that loosens the nails can significantly decrease the integrity of these important connections.

Picture 1

Handrail not Graspable

Good example of **a handrail that is not graspable**. In addition, this handrail does not comply with hand rail size and shape requirements.

See Chapter 6 for handrail size and shape requirements.

> Note: While the term guardrail (also guard rail) is often used, the IRC refers to this part of the structure as a guard.

The remaining deck systems are important, but are less likely to be a major factor in causing injuries. Examples of these systems include: deck footings, support posts, and framing components such as beams and joists.

This book will not make you an experienced deck inspector, and it will not give you instructions on how to build a deck. Rather, this book is intended to give you the information you need to identify common deck problems.

In most cases, the smart move is to hire a qualified contractor or home inspector to help you determine your best option. In addition, always check with the local authority regarding permits and inspections, and be certain to follow the guidelines.

Decks are often undertaken as a do-it-yourself (DIY) project. Given correct attention to modern design specifications and workmanship, this can be a fine project for homeowners. A lack of knowledge, however, can lead to disaster. In fact, deck failure can cause serious injury or death. Decks are often the weakest structural component in the home.

Dr. Don Bender, Weyerhaeuser Professor, Washington State University

2

What is a Deck?

That seems like a silly question. A deck is that wood platform that is usually found at the back or side of the house. Well, that is one type of deck. Other structures that are not called decks (balcony, landing, porch) may actually be constructed in the same way as a deck, and are subject to the same disaster potential.

A deck can be a stairway and covered space at the front door; in which case it is usually called a front porch or a stoop. A deck can be a stairway and a landing leading to a door. A deck can have a roof and be enclosed by screens; in which case it is usually called a screened porch. These are only a few examples of deck-like structures.

For the purposes of this book, we are going to define a deck as follows. A deck is made from wood. The deck floor may be a composite material, but the structure is wood, usually pressure-treated wood or a naturally durable wood such as Redwood. A deck is supported by posts at some or all points. The posts are usually wood but are sometimes steel or other materials such as bricks.

What are structures that might be considered decks, but are not decks in this book?

We will call a structure that extends out from the house wall and is supported only at the house a cantilevered balcony. We will call a structure that serves as a roof for an area below a balcony. We will call a structure made from concrete, pavers, and similar solid materials a patio.

We define decks in this way because the purpose of this book is to give you simple guidelines that can help you determine if your deck is a candidate for a disaster. Structures like balconies are also candidates for disaster, but important parts of balconies are often concealed.

Evaluation of these complex structures requires professional knowledge and experience. Hire a qualified contractor or home inspector to help you determine your best options.

3

Flashing

What is flashing?

Flashing is a permanent, low maintenance barrier that stops water from flowing to where it could cause damage. Flashing is different from sealants such as caulk and roofing cement. Sealants may require replacement in as little as a year. Flashing, when properly installed, should last for the life of the deck. Sealants may be used in addition to flashing, but sealants should not be used as a substitute for properly installed flashing.

Flashing for decks built **before 2004** is usually aluminum or galvanized steel. Both are acceptable materials, but both can degrade over time, fail, and require replacement.

Flashing for decks built <u>since 2004</u> should be made from copper, one of the new flexible polymer materials, or PVC. Galvanized steel may be used, but this material can rust over time. Aluminum should not be used because it can degrade rapidly when exposed to the preservative chemicals used to treat deck lumber.

Why is flashing important?

Wood rot caused by water is a leading cause of catastrophic deck failure. Water that enters the house around the deck and around doors that open on to the deck can damage other materials in the house and provide moisture that mold needs to grow. Water damage to the deck or house structure can weaken them to the point of catastrophic failure.

Unfortunately, a spectacular balcony failure in California, and a deck failure in North Carolina, both in 2015, have been attributed to water damage. The failure in California resulted in several fatalities, and the failure in North Carolina resulted in several serious injuries. Research of earlier reported incidents (See Appendix I) often lists water damage as one of the causes of the failure.

Picture 2 shows a severely damaged band joist that was near failure. (There had been a deck attached to the band joist shown. At some point, cosmetic improvements had been made to the deck, but there had been no structural review.)

Picture 2

Water Damaged Band Joist and Sill Plate

The band joist serves a crucial function. It supports the vertical and horizontal loads imposed by the deck on the house.

Where should deck flashing be located?

Deck flashing should be located at two places:

> (1) at any place where the deck touches the house, and

> (2) at doors that open on to the deck.

Door flashing is required whether or not the door opens on to a deck; however, flashing for doors that open onto a deck should be integrated with the deck flashing.

Deck flashing is not required for free-standing decks that do not touch the house.

What are some common deck flashing defects?

> (1) no flashing between deck and house,

> (2) no flashing at and under deck door threshold,

> (3) no flashing or sealant where deck parts (such as guardrails) penetrate wall coverings,

(4) flashing with gaps or seams that allow water to get behind or around the flashing as per **Picture 2,** and **Picture 3**,

Picture 3

Gap between Deck Flashing and Door Threshold

(5) damaged and deteriorated flashing,

(6) flashing that relies on caulk, other sealants, or fasteners such as nails to secure the flashing to the wall,

(7) flashing installed in front of wall coverings instead of behind them,

(8) flashing that is installed behind the deck ledger board instead of on top. Note that this flashing method is allowed in some parts of the country and may work if properly installed.

Where should I look for water damage around decks?

The most common location for water damage around decks is around doors that open on to the deck.

The next most common location is anywhere that the deck is attached to the house.

Water damage usually presents as dark stains and as soft wood that you can easily penetrate with a screwdriver. Dark stains on the outside deck boards are normal and are rarely a concern. Dark stains inside the house indicate that water has found its way in. These stains are a concern.

See **Picture 4**.

Picture 4

Water Stains Inside the House

This picture shows the water infiltration caused by the flashing defect in **Picture 3**.

Look where the deck is attached to the house. Look inside the house where the deck is attached and any other place where the deck touches the house. Pay special attention to places where bolts or screws penetrate the interior wood. You may need to move insulation or ceiling tiles to look at these inside areas. If the inside area has a permanent finished ceiling, such as drywall, look for irregular shaped brown stains on the drywall.

Look on the exterior side of doors that open on to the deck, especially under the door and at the corners where the vertical jambs and the horizontal sill meet. Look inside on the floor around the door, especially at the corners.

How should deck flashing be installed?

Most flashing should be integrated with other materials so that the material above is lapped over the material below. This creates a drainage plane like shingles on a roof. Water that hits this drainage plane should drain harmlessly away from the house.

Figure 1 shows a side view of the current best practice for installing deck flashing.

Note the two types of flashing:

> (1) a water-resistive membrane between the deck ledger on the right and the band joist on the left, and

> (2) L flashing on top of the deck ledger.

The L flashing may be installed above the deck floor boards too, but this installation method is not as aesthetically pleasing.

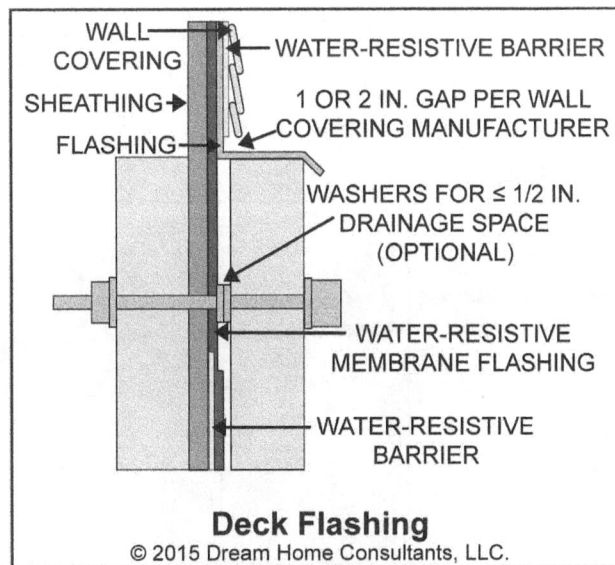

Figure 1

Current best practice for installing deck flashing.

Also note that above the ledger, the flashing is lapped under the water-resistive barrier that should be under the wall covering. The flashing is lapped over the water-resistive barrier under the deck ledger.

Figure 2 shows the current best practice for installing pan flashing at the deck door.

Pan flashing is essential for diverting water that might enter under the door sill or at the sill edges. Note that this installation takes place before the door is installed.

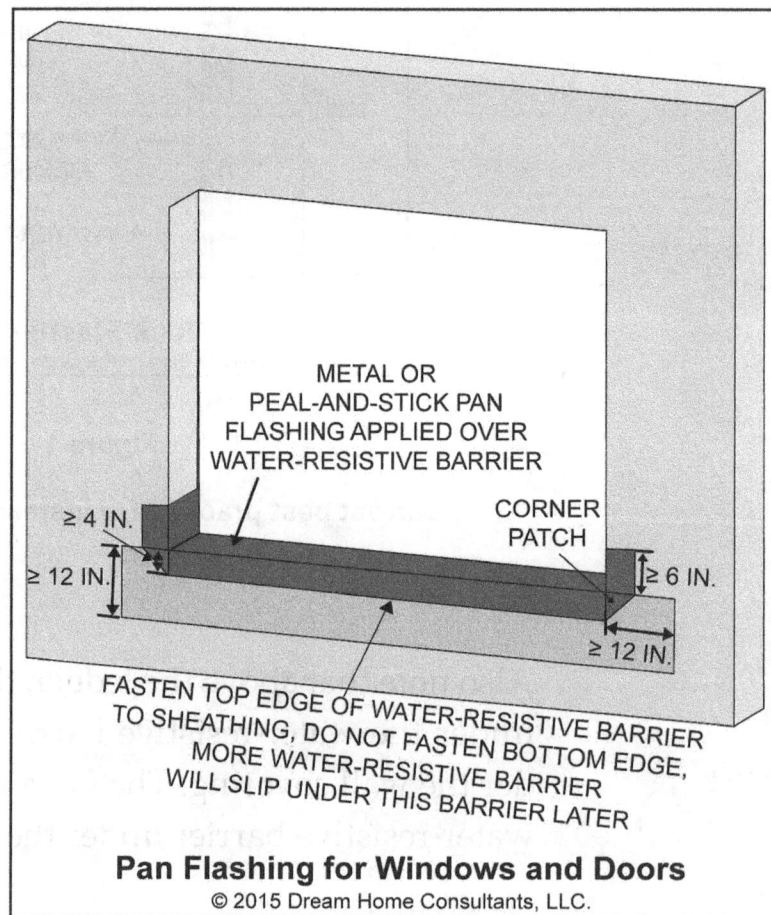

METAL OR
PEAL-AND-STICK PAN
FLASHING APPLIED OVER
WATER-RESISTIVE BARRIER

CORNER
PATCH

≥ 4 IN.

≥ 12 IN.

≥ 6 IN.

≥ 12 IN.

FASTEN TOP EDGE OF WATER-RESISTIVE BARRIER
TO SHEATHING, DO NOT FASTEN BOTTOM EDGE,
MORE WATER-RESISTIVE BARRIER
WILL SLIP UNDER THIS BARRIER LATER

Pan Flashing for Windows and Doors

© 2015 Dream Home Consultants, LLC.

Figure 2

Pan Flashing for Windows and Doors

Figure 3 shows the current best practice for the side and top flashing at the deck door. **Figure 2** and **Figure 3** show windows, but the installation applies to doors too.

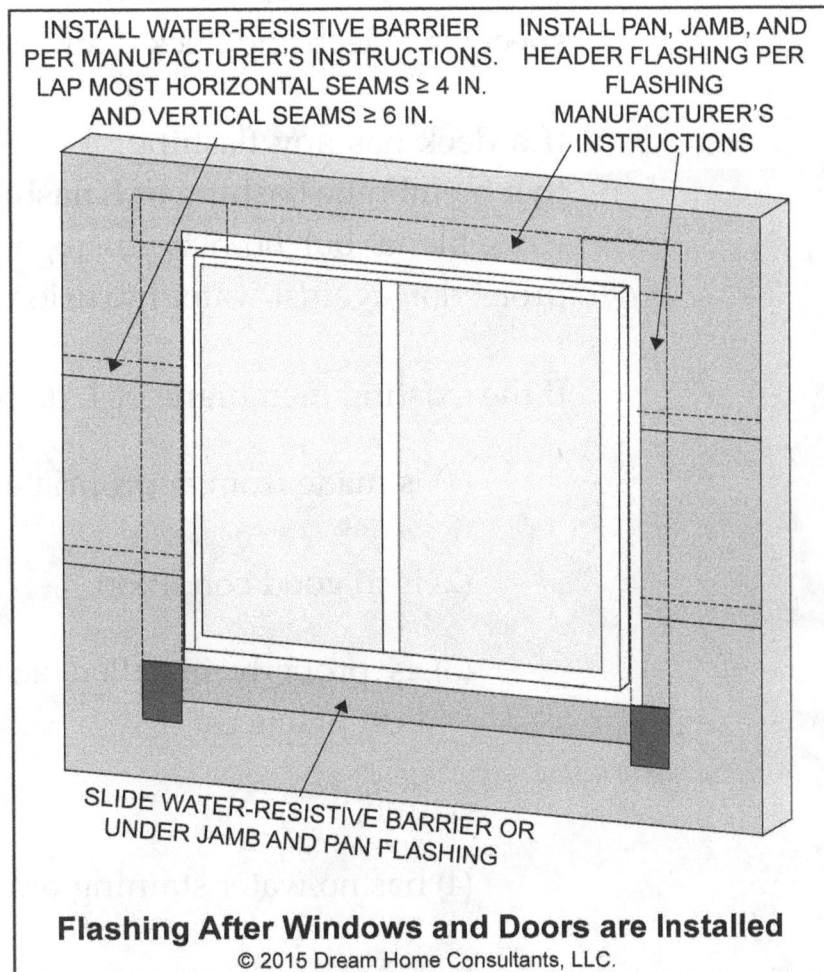

INSTALL WATER-RESISTIVE BARRIER PER MANUFACTURER'S INSTRUCTIONS. LAP MOST HORIZONTAL SEAMS ≥ 4 IN. AND VERTICAL SEAMS ≥ 6 IN.

INSTALL PAN, JAMB, AND HEADER FLASHING PER FLASHING MANUFACTURER'S INSTRUCTIONS

SLIDE WATER-RESISTIVE BARRIER OR UNDER JAMB AND PAN FLASHING

Flashing After Windows and Doors are Installed
© 2015 Dream Home Consultants, LLC.

Figure 3

Drainage Plane for Windows and Doors

What should I do if my deck or deck door is not flashed according to best practices?

Few decks or deck doors, especially older ones, will have flashing installed according to best practices. Whether this is a problem for you depends on which of several possible situations you find when you inspect your deck and deck door flashing.

If a deck has any flashing, it will probably have either membrane flashing or L flashing. Either type can work alone, but both types together provide better protection against water intrusion.

If the existing membrane or L deck flashing:

(1) is made from appropriate material,

(2) is in good condition,

(3) is properly installed according to current best practices,

and,

(4) has no water staining or damage,

then there may be no need to change anything. **You should inspect your deck, as previously stated, at least once per year to look for evidence of water intrusion.**

If you find water staining or damage inside the house or at the deck ledger, then you will need to find the water source and stop the water intrusion. This may not be easy. Water staining and damage can appear far from the water source.

If you find no deck flashing, you should install some even if you do not find water staining or damage. Sometimes, minor water intrusion takes time to produce visible stains and damage. Note that retrofitting pan flashing and ledger flashing at an existing deck can be a difficult and involved process.

The steps you will need to take to repair faulty deck flashing or to install deck flashing where none exists will be different for each situation and are beyond the scope of this book. You should hire a qualified contractor or home inspector to help you determine the appropriate steps for your situation.

If a deck door has any flashing, it probably does not have properly installed pan flashing. If you see no flashing under the door threshold, the door has no pan flashing. Sealant may have been applied under the door threshold when the door was installed, but this is difficult to determine visually.

If your deck door has no pan flashing under the door threshold, applying sealant under the threshold can be an acceptable temporary solution in some cases. Read and follow the sealant manufacturer's instructions when selecting and installing a sealant under the door threshold.

Applying sealant as a substitute for pan flashing assumes that there is at least 1 ½ inches between the bottom of the door threshold and the deck. This distance is necessary to help prevent wind-blown rain and water from infiltrating under the door.

More distance may be necessary in climates where snow can drift against the door. The distance between the door threshold and the deck should be at least the likely snow depth, but not more than 7 ¾ inches (distance will vary according to local requirements) below the top of the door threshold.

Free-standing Decks: An Alternative

Flashing can be difficult to install correctly, especially at an existing deck when the doors and wall coverings are already installed. Sealants are better than nothing, but are a last resort to be used when proper flashing cannot be installed. Dropping the deck several inches below the door threshold can make properly attaching the deck ledger to the house difficult or impossible. There is an alternative that eliminates all of these difficulties: the free-standing deck.

A free-standing deck is not attached to the house at all. It is supported on all sides by footings and posts. A free-standing deck is usually more expensive to build; however, the advantages of avoiding water damage problems and of avoiding deck failures caused by improper ledger connection to the house can compensate for the higher initial cost.

A free-standing deck can be a great alternative when building a new deck and when replacing an existing deck. In the real world, however, many people find themselves with an existing deck that does not need to be replaced, but is improperly flashed.

Often a free-standing deck is not a realistic alternative in this common situation. So what should you do?

If you believe that your deck is improperly flashed or if you are not sure, you should consult with a qualified contractor or home inspector to determine your best course of action.

4

Deck Ledger Attachment to House

What does deck ledger attachment to the house mean?

Most decks use the house as one of the structural supports. To provide this support, a board called a deck ledger is usually attached to a part of the floor system of the house called a band joist or a rim board. This connection between the deck and the house is an essential element of the structural stability of a deck. Flashing helps maintain this structural stability by preserving the integrity of the wood and the connectors; however, flashing does no good if the connectors are improperly installed.

Figure 4 (see next page) illustrates some terms we will use in this and other chapters.

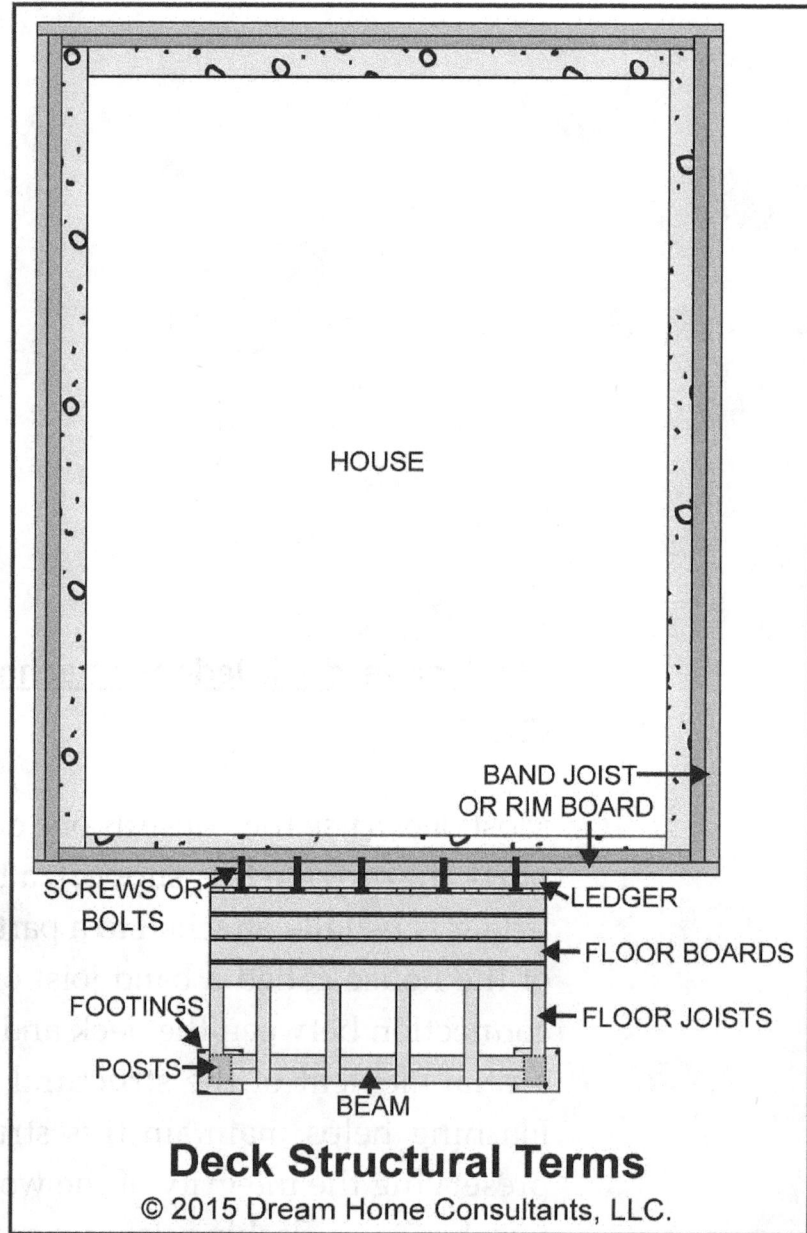

Deck Structural Terms
© 2015 Dream Home Consultants, LLC.

Figure 4

Deck Structural Terms

As early as 2003, the International Residential Code (IRC 2003, R502.2.1 Decks) stated that: Where supported by attachment to an exterior wall, decks shall be positively anchored to the primary structure and designed for both vertical and lateral loads as applicable. **Such attachment shall not be accomplished by the use of toenails or nails subject to withdrawal...**

Note that almost all nails are subject to withdrawal. This is why nails may not be used as the only method of securing a deck ledger to the house.

For many years the IRC (design criteria) stated that "buildings and structures, and all parts thereof, shall be constructed to support safely all loads... ." This means that deck builders must consider all loads that may be imposed on the deck, including horizontal (lateral) loads and vertical loads. The deck must be able to support these loads when the deck is new and when it has been exposed to years of rain and snow that can weaken the lumber and the fasteners.

Deck ledgers should be attached to the band joist or rim board using hot-dipped galvanized steel or stainless steel machine bolts (not carriage bolts) or lag screws that are at least ½ inch diameter. Older decks may have been attached to the house using only nails. **This is a serious defect that should be corrected immediately.** Decks attached using only nails are much more likely to fall down compared to decks attached using bolts or screws. See **Picture 5**.

Picture 5

Deck Ledger Secured using only Nails

Why are nails not allowed for deck ledger attachment?

Recent research into deck collapses has determined that most collapses occur because the deck pulls away from the house in a horizontal direction. Collapse in a vertical direction also occurs, but this is not as common. One reason why horizontal failures are more common is that fasteners such as nails have good resistance to breaking in the vertical direction, but they have very low resistance to pulling out from wood in the horizontal direction. A safe deck that is attached to the house needs a good connection in both the horizontal and vertical directions. Properly installed bolts or screws can provide the necessary connection; nails cannot.

How should a deck ledger be attached to the house?

Connecting a deck ledger to the house is complicated because there are many ways to build a house and many ways to conect a deck ledger to a house. For example, the floor system in older houses used lumber floor joists such as 2x10s. Newer houses may use wood I joists or trusses as the floor system. The floor system of the house may be perpendicular to the band joist or rim board, or it may be parallel to the band joist or rim board. Floor system orientation can be important to keep the deck ledger from pulling the band joist or the rim board off of the house. Some people may want to connect the deck ledger directly to a concrete block foundation or to a poured concrete foundation. All of these situations present different challenges for making a safe connection between the deck ledger and the house.

A safe connection between the deck ledger and the house requires installing the correct type and quantity of bolts, screws, or connectors. There are specific rules about how, where, and how many bolts, screws, or connectors should be installed. These rules depend on factors such as the length of the deck joists, the orientation of the band joist or rim board to the floor system of the house, and the material to which the deck ledger is connected (e.g., wood band joist or concrete block). These rules are available from sources listed in the references section and are beyond the scope of this book.

These general rules assume that the deck ledger is connected to a lumber band joist or to a rim board and that the house floor system is perpendicular to the band joist or rim board. Other connection methods and other materials may be safe, but a qualified contractor or home inspector should evaluate them.

The deck ledger should not be attached through any exterior wall covering such as siding, stucco, or brick. The deck ledger should be no more than 1 inch from the band joist or rim board. This 1 inch includes wall sheathing, flashing, and any drainage spacing. **Fig-**

ure 5 is a summary of current best practice for attaching the deck ledger to a band joist or rim board.

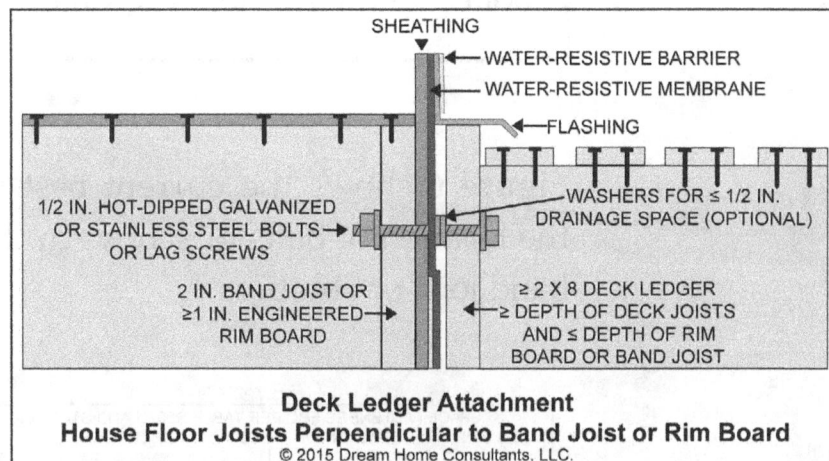

Deck Ledger Attachment
House Floor Joists Perpendicular to Band Joist or Rim Board
© 2015 Dream Home Consultants, LLC.

Figure 5

A post-deck collapse inspection revealed that the main support affixing the deck to the house---called a ledger board---was attached to particle board with only a few nails inserted through vinyl siding...(this collapse resulted in one death and several serious injuries) www.sbjlaw.com

...(the victim) fractured a vertebra and ruptured his colon. He had to spend almost four months in the hospital... City officials later found that the deck had been nailed to the house instead of bolted to the frame. www.hamptonroads.com

Figure 6 shows the current best practice regarding the location of bolts or screws in the deck ledger and band joist or rim board.

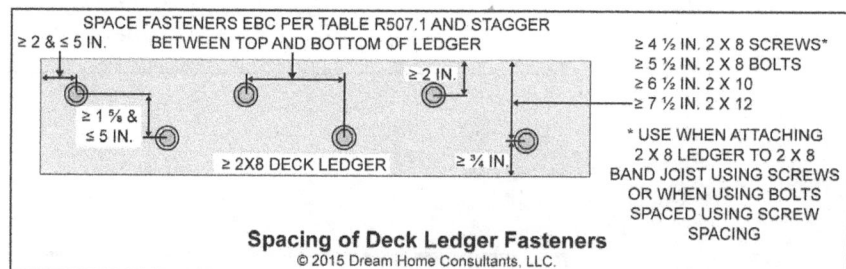

Figure 6

When the deck ledger is attached to the house floor system, the ledger should be attached to a band joist that is at least 2 inches **nominal** thickness, for example, 2x10, which is 1 ½ inches **actual** thickness, or to an engineered lumber rim board that is at least 1 inch **actual** thickness. The band joist or rim board must bear directly on the foundation of the home or on something, such as a framed wall, that bears directly on the foundation. Connection to a projection beyond the foundation, such as a bay window or a wood-framed chimney, is not allowed. The floor joists for the floor system of the house should be solid wood lumber or engineered wood I joists that are perpendicular to the band joist or rim board.

What are some common deck ledger attachment defects?

(1) deck ledger is attached using only nails,

(2) deck ledger is attached through exterior wall coverings,

(3) deck ledger is attached to a cantilevered structure such as a bay window,

(4) deck ledger, band joist, rim board, or connectors are damaged and do not provide a secure connection,

(5) no washers are installed on bolts or screws,

(6) bolts or screws are too small,

(7) bolts or screws are too close to the edge of the deck ledger, band joist, or rim board,

(8) band joist or rim board is not the proper material or size,

(9) house floor joists are parallel to the band joist or rim board.

What should I do if my deck ledger is not properly attached to the house?

Deck ledger attachment is one of the most important safety issues for decks. Many, if not most, catastrophic deck failures are the result of deck ledger attachment defects.

If you believe that your deck is improperly attached or if you are not sure, you should consult with a qualified contractor or home inspector to determine your best course of action.

5

Stairs

How are deck stairs made?

Deck stairs are usually made from 2x10 or 2x12 lumber called stringers. Triangle-shaped pieces are cut from the stringers to form the vertical parts of the steps called risers and horizontal parts of the steps called treads.

(1) Deck stairs should end at the top and bottom in a solid landing.

(2) Deck stairs may have one or more landings in the middle.

Figure 7 shows the current best practices for building deck stairs and attaching them to the deck.

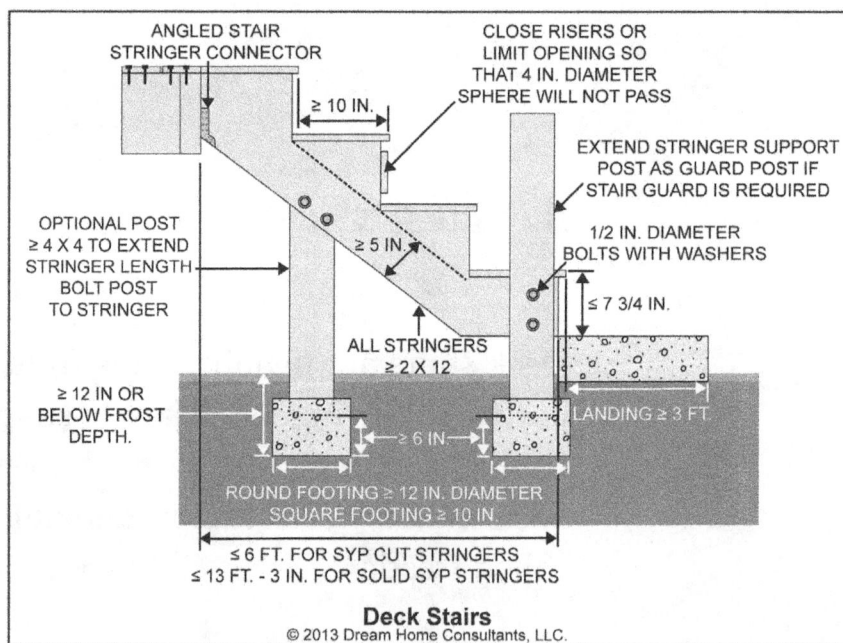

Figure 7

Figure 8 shows an alternative method for building deck stairs and attaching them to the deck. This method may not be accepted in all areas.

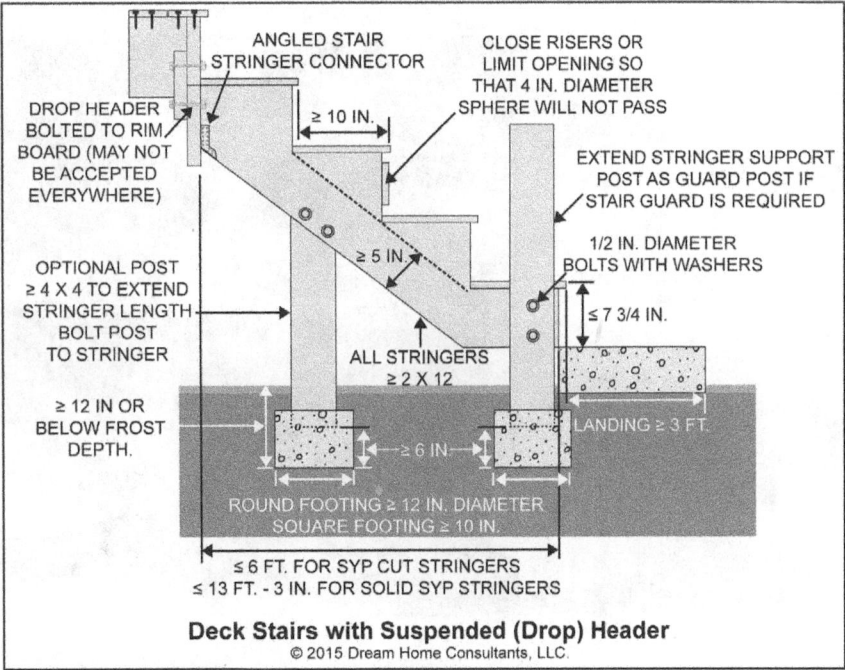

Deck Stairs with Suspended (Drop) Header
© 2015 Dream Home Consultants, LLC.

Figure 8

How do deck stairs fail?

Deck stairs usually fail by pulling away from the deck and falling. The usual cause of the failure is an improper or damaged connection between the stringers and the deck. See **Picture 6.**

Picture 6

Stair Failure

Factors contributing to failure include stringers that are weak due to excessively deep riser and tread cuts, excessive distance between stringer supports, and lack of a solid landing at the bottom. Weak and improperly supported stringers can bend excessively when walked on, and over time pull the stringer connections loose from the deck.

What are some common stair defects?

(1) stringer plumb (vertical) cut does not fully bear on deck or other structural support (See **Picture 7.**),

© 2013 Dream Home Consultants, LLC.

Picture 7

Inadequate Stringer bearing at Deck

(2) stringer is inadequately attached to deck using only nails (See **Picture 8.**),

Picture 8

Toe Nailed Stringer pulling away from Deck

(3) stringer tread cut is cut too deep into solid wood (See **Picture 9.**),

Picture 9

Stringer Excessively Cut

(4) risers too tall, riser height uneven,

(5) treads not deep enough, tread depth uneven,

(6) stringer too long between supports,

(7) no landing at bottom of stairs,

> Lack of a bottom landing is a safety deficiency; however, building codes in some states do not require a landing at the bottom of deck stairs.

(8) deteriorated or loose tread boards.

How should stairs be built and attached to the deck?

Stringers should be built using pressure treated 2x12 Southern Yellow Pine or wood with similar properties. The minimum depth of uncut wood should be 5 inches. Note that saw cuts into the wood reduce the depth of the uncut wood, so measurement is to the end of the deepest saw cut. See **Picture 9**.

The entire plumb cut (vertical cut) of the stringers should bear on support at the deck. The stringers may be set as an extension of the deck landing as shown in **Figure 7** or the stringers may be dropped below the deck to make one riser up to the deck.

As shown in **Figure 8**, if the stringers are dropped, a secure suspended (drop) header must be provided to support the plumb cut of the stringer. Note that drop headers may not be allowed in all areas.

The stringers should be connected to the deck using angled joist hangers. Other connection methods, including nails, are common and are still allowed in many areas. Nails should not be used to connect stringers because they may withdraw as shown in **Picture 6** and in **Picture 8.**

Proper riser height and tread depth are important for safe stairs as is consistency of these measurements between risers and treads. See **Figure 7** and **Figure 8** for the maximum riser height and minimum tread depth. The riser height and tread depth should be consistent within ⅜ inch between any two risers and treads. Note that riser height, tread depth and allowed inconsistency may be different in different areas.

What should I do if there are problems with my deck stairs?

Adding support posts under stringers that are weak or too long can be a good way to address these problems. Adding joist hangers at the stringer connections to the deck can often be done without too much difficulty. Correcting riser height and tread depth problems usually requires replacing the stringers.

If you believe there are problems with your deck stairs or if you are not sure, you should consult with a qualified contractor or home inspector to determine your best course of action.

6

Handrails and Guardrails

What are handrails and guardrails?

Handrails are an important safety feature that provide a graspable surface for those who use the stairs. A surface with a size and shape that can be easily grasped is important, especially for children, small adults, and those with reduced mobility.

Guardrails are an important safety feature that help prevent falls from heights. Guardrails at the sides of stairs often serve as both handrails and guardrails.

NOTE: Guardrails are referred to as guards in the International Residential Code (IRC).

Where are handrails and guardrails required?

Handrails are required on one side of stairs with four or more risers; however, handrails are recommended for all stairs regardless of the number of risers. The handrail should be continuous from the first to the last riser.

Guardrails are required when a walking surface, such as a deck, is more than 30 inches above another area. Guardrails are required on the open (not enclosed by a wall) sides of stairs with risers that are more than 30 inches above another area. If both sides of the stairs are open, then a guardrail is required on both sides.

What should handrails look like?

It has been determined that only certain handrail shapes and sizes provide a graspable surface for most people. **Figure 9** shows examples of acceptable handrails.

A piece of 2x4 lumber is often installed as a handrail. See **Picture 1**. This type of handrail is not one of the shapes shown in **Figure 9,** is not graspable, and is not safe.

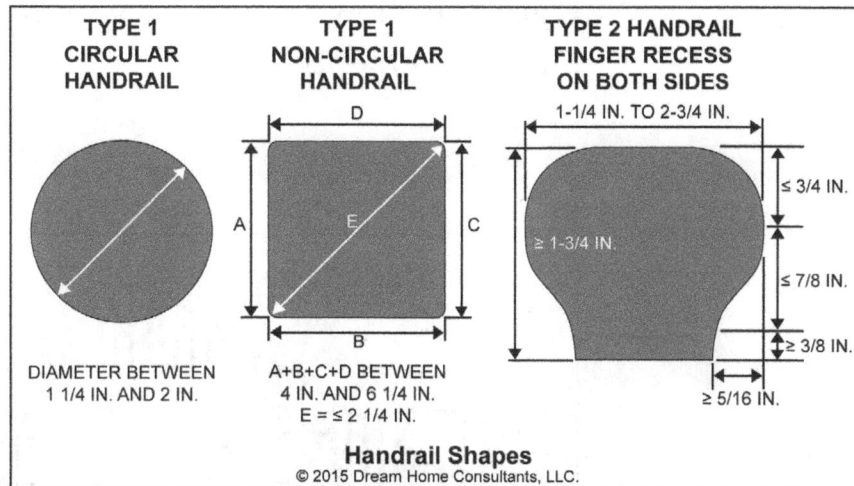

```
TYPE 1                TYPE 1              TYPE 2 HANDRAIL
CIRCULAR            NON-CIRCULAR         FINGER RECESS
HANDRAIL             HANDRAIL            ON BOTH SIDES
                                     1-1/4 IN. TO 2-3/4 IN.
```

DIAMETER BETWEEN   A+B+C+D BETWEEN
1 1/4 IN. AND 2 IN.   4 IN. AND 6 1/4 IN.
                            E = ≤ 2 1/4 IN.

Handrail Shapes
© 2015 Dream Home Consultants, LLC.

Figure 9

What should guardrails look like?

Properly installed guardrails should provide these safety features:

(1) high enough to prevent someone from falling over the guardrail (36 inches tall in most areas),

(2) strong enough so that someone cannot push it over or go through it,

(3) narrow enough openings so that a child's head cannot become trapped between the openings.

Figure 10 shows a summary of guardrail and handrail requirements.

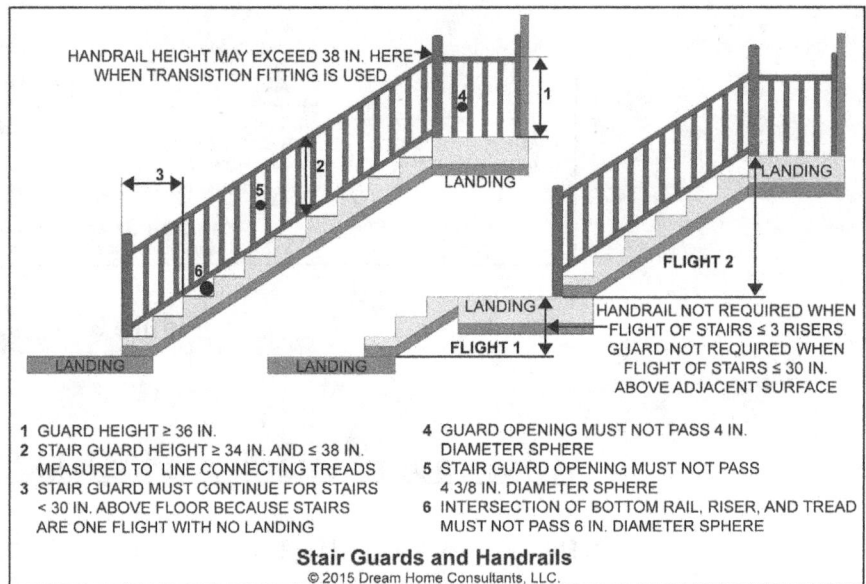

HANDRAIL HEIGHT MAY EXCEED 38 IN. HERE WHEN TRANSISTION FITTING IS USED

LANDING

LANDING

FLIGHT 2

LANDING

LANDING

LANDING

LANDING

FLIGHT 1

HANDRAIL NOT REQUIRED WHEN FLIGHT OF STAIRS ≤ 3 RISERS
GUARD NOT REQUIRED WHEN FLIGHT OF STAIRS ≤ 30 IN. ABOVE ADJACENT SURFACE

1 GUARD HEIGHT ≥ 36 IN.
2 STAIR GUARD HEIGHT ≥ 34 IN. AND ≤ 38 IN. MEASURED TO LINE CONNECTING TREADS
3 STAIR GUARD MUST CONTINUE FOR STAIRS < 30 IN. ABOVE FLOOR BECAUSE STAIRS ARE ONE FLIGHT WITH NO LANDING

4 GUARD OPENING MUST NOT PASS 4 IN. DIAMETER SPHERE
5 STAIR GUARD OPENING MUST NOT PASS 4 3/8 IN. DIAMETER SPHERE
6 INTERSECTION OF BOTTOM RAIL, RISER, AND TREAD MUST NOT PASS 6 IN. DIAMETER SPHERE

Stair Guards and Handrails
© 2015 Dream Home Consultants, LLC.

Figure 10

Strong guardrail support posts are at least 4x4 and are not cut or notched where attached to the deck.

> Many years of observation has shown that moisture cycles will typically cause cracks to develop and propagate, parallel to the grain, from the corner of the notch. This may not be apparent when the post is first installed, but it happens gradually over time. Loferski, et al, 2005.

Picture 10 shows an example of a notched guard post.

Picture 10

Guardrail Post Improperly Notched and Secured with Nails

While the IRC does address performance requirements for guards (guardrails), the IRC does not address the issue of how to attach guard posts. The posts should be attached to the deck using a bolted bracket as shown in **Figure 11.**

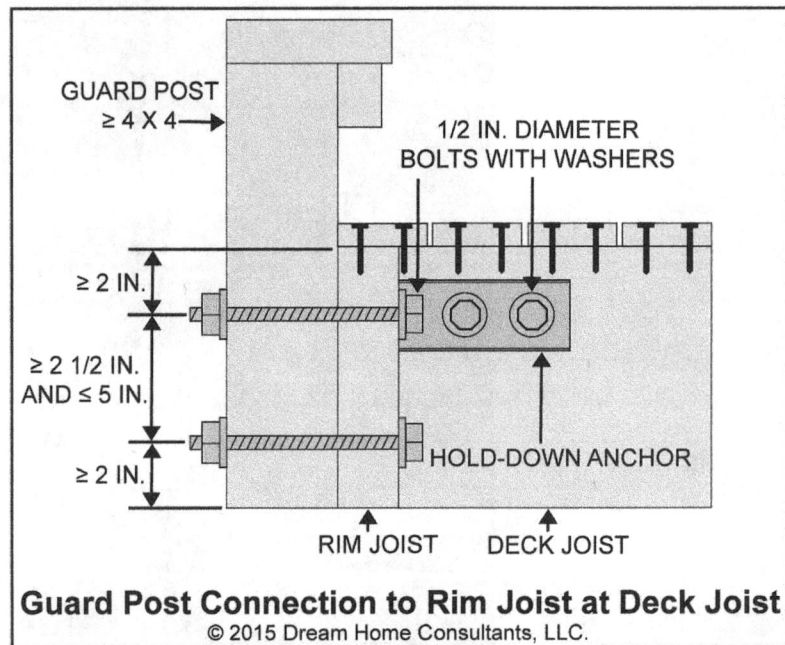

Guard Post Connection to Rim Joist at Deck Joist
© 2015 Dream Home Consultants, LLC.

Figure 11

Posts that are attached using bolts without brackets are allowed by government inspectors in many areas, but this connection may not provide satisfactory strength over the life of the deck. The posts should be no more than six feet apart.

It is important to reiterate regarding deck post attachment that just because something is allowed by government inspectors does not make it a good idea. Government inspectors are limited to enforcing existing building codes. Building codes are slow to change and may not reflect best (and safe) practices.

What are some common handrail and guardrail defects?

(1) no handrail or guardrail,

(2) handrail grip surface wrong size or shape,

(3) loose handrail or guardrail,

(4) deteriorated handrail, splinters,

(5) handrail not continuous over entire flight of stairs,

(6) guardrail not tall enough,

(7) guardrail support posts notched at attachment to deck,

(8) guardrail support posts nailed or screwed to deck,

(9) guardrail vertical components (balusters) spaced too far apart (more than 4 inches),

(10) guardrail support posts too far apart.

What should I do if there are problems with my deck handrails or guardrails?

Proper size and shape handrails can usually be added to deck stairs without difficulty. Full size (4x4) guardrail support posts can usually be secured using brackets without difficulty. Problems such as notched guardrail support posts, and support posts and vertical components that are spaced too far apart will usually require replacement of the improperly installed posts and components.

If you believe there are problems with your deck handrails or guardrails or if you are not sure, you should consult with a qualified contractor or home inspector to determine your best course of action.

Framing

What is deck framing?

For the purposes of this book, deck framing includes components such as floor joists and beams, deck floor boards, joist hangers, nails and screws, and deck braces. **Figure 4** in Chapter 4 shows some deck framing components.

Unfortunately, some deck failures are caused by deterioration of the wood. Wood deterioration is often caused by water infiltration and improper flashing. Also, especially in unpermitted work, material not rated for exterior use or ground contact is sometimes used. For this reason it is important to follow best practices and to obtain the required building permits.

What are some common deck framing defects?

(1) floor joists are too long between supports,

(2) floor joists extended too far (cantilevered) past supports,

(3) beam is too long between supports,

(4) joints between pieces of built-up beams are not supported at a post,

(5) joists are not supported by ledger or joist hanger,

(6) joist hangers, screws, and nails are not hot-dipped galvanized steel or stainless steel,

(7) deck framing materials are damaged or deteriorated,

(8) deck braces are not installed or are improperly installed,

(9) deck materials that are not rated for ground contact are touching the ground, or are too near the ground,

(10) joist hangers are improperly installed.

Picture 11

Joist Hanger Improperly Installed

How should deck floor joists and beams be installed?

Deck floor joists are limited in how far they may run between supports. They are also limited in how far they can project past supports. **Figure 12** shows these limits. Note that the maximum projection beyond support (called a cantilever) can vary among jurisdictions. Consult DCA6-12 and your local building inspector for more information.

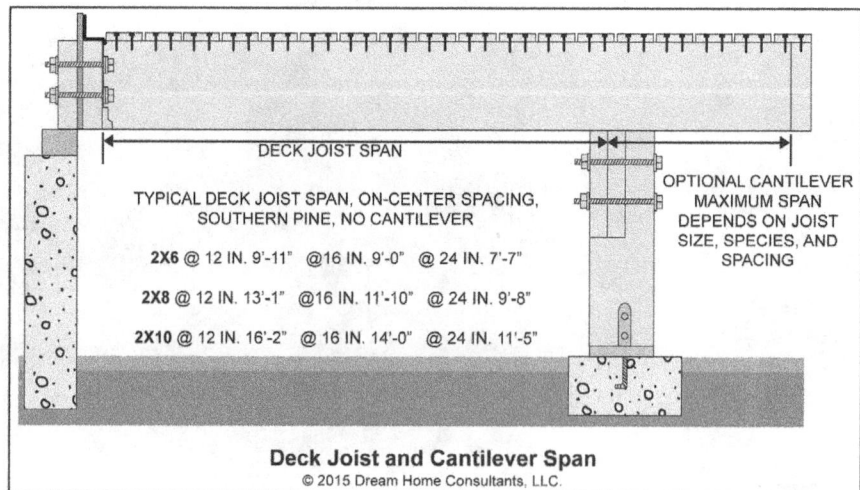

Deck Joist and Cantilever Span
© 2015 Dream Home Consultants, LLC.

Figure 12

These limits help keep joists that are too long from bending and from placing stress on other deck components that can cause them to fail. Deck floor joists should be supported by a joist hanger, or on top of a beam as shown in **Figure 13.** Deck floor joists are frequently supported by a 2x2 strip of wood that is also (confusingly) called a ledger. While using a ledger to support deck floor joists is common practice and allowed in many areas, it is another example of where what is allowed may not reflect best or safe practice.

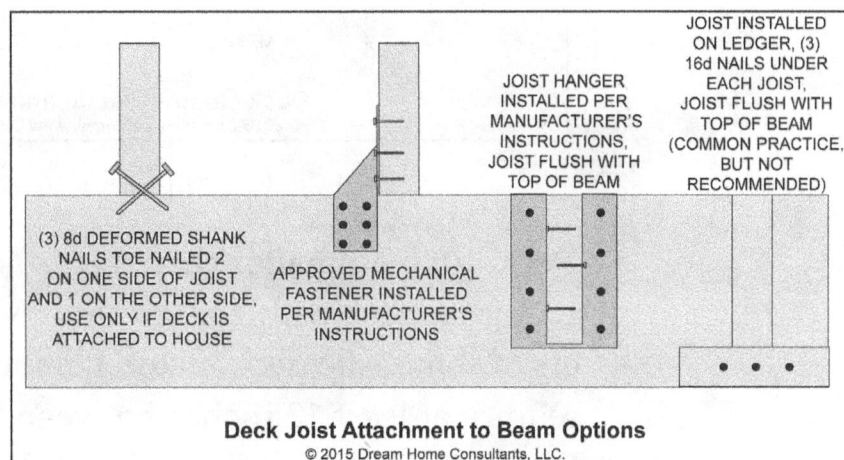

Deck Joist Attachment to Beam Options
© 2015 Dream Home Consultants, LLC.

Figure 13

Deck beams are also limited in how far they may run between supports. Deck beams are often made from multiple pieces of lumber. The joint between two pieces of the beam should occur at a support post. **Figure 14** shows these requirements.

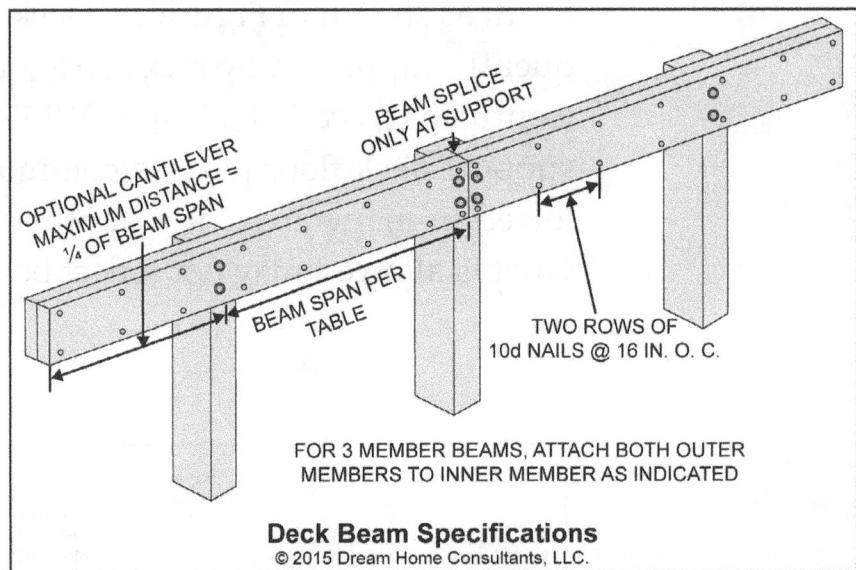

Deck Beam Specifications
© 2015 Dream Home Consultants, LLC.

Figure 14

Deck lumber smaller than 4x4 is sometimes not rated for contact with the ground. Many manufacturers of composite deck materials, such as floor boards, require at least 12 inches between the materials and the ground. It is a good idea to leave a few inches, or whatever the manufacturer recommends, between deck materials and the ground.

How should joist hangers, nails, and screws be installed?

Joist hangers, nails, and screws (and any other products) should be installed according to manufacturer's instructions. These instructions are easy to find on the internet. For example, a 2x8 deck floor joist should be supported by a joist hanger designed for use with a 2x8 and should be fastened using fasteners specified by the joist hanger manufacturer. The joist hanger should be made from galvanized steel or stainless steel and should be listed for exterior use. Joist hangers for interior use will rust and weaken if used outdoors.

The heads of screws and nails should be installed flush with the wood or joist hanger. Nails and screws that are set too deep create a water trap that can damage the wood.

Nails should be deformed shank type, except where another type of nail is specified by the manufacturer of a product, such as the joist hanger. Deformed shank nails have rings or a screw pattern on the nail to help it grip the wood and resist pulling out of the wood.

How should deck bracing be installed?

A deck is very heavy, but it can be moved by the wind, by earthquakes, and even by people. Movement stresses the nails, bolts, and screws that hold the deck up and hold it together. These stresses can contribute to catastrophic deck collapse.

Deck bracing helps reduce deck movement. Deck bracing is a relatively new requirement, so you will not see it on older decks. Fortunately, deck bracing is easy and inexpensive to add to existing decks and to install on new decks.

Deck bracing is recommended for decks that are more than 2 feet above the ground. Bracing for decks that are attached to the house should be installed as shown in **Figure 15.**

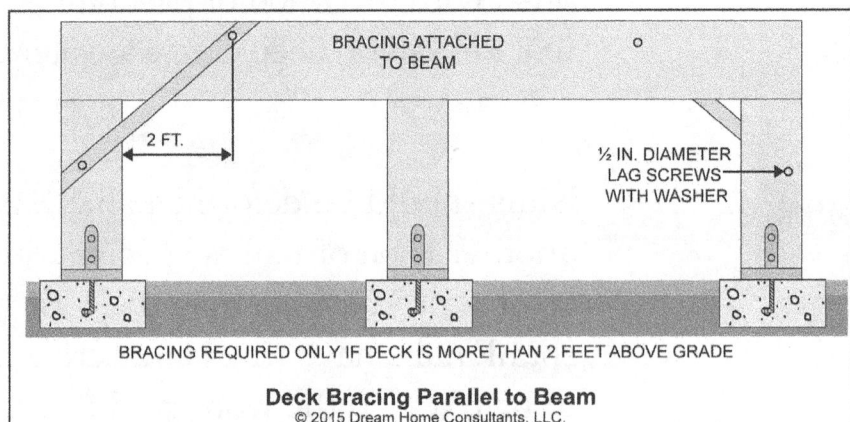

BRACING ATTACHED TO BEAM

2 FT.

½ IN. DIAMETER LAG SCREWS WITH WASHER

BRACING REQUIRED ONLY IF DECK IS MORE THAN 2 FEET ABOVE GRADE

Deck Bracing Parallel to Beam
© 2015 Dream Home Consultants, LLC.

Figure 15

What should I do if there are problems with my deck framing?

Resolving deck framing problems may require more knowledge and experience than most people have.

If you believe that your deck has framing problems or if you are not sure, you should consult with a qualified contractor or home inspector to determine your best course of action.

8

Support Posts and Footings

What are support posts and footings?

Most decks should be raised above the ground at least a few inches, and often a foot or more to allow the lumber to dry out between moisture events. Support posts raise the deck above the ground. They run between the deck and the footing (concrete that is placed in the earth).

Picture 12

Good idea? No.

Do not put a support post in front of a garage door.

Support posts are usually made from pressure treated Southern Pine, other softwood, or a naturally decay resistant lumber such as Redwood. The recommend minimum support post size for decks up to 14 feet above the ground is 6x6. Support posts made from 4x4 are acceptable for decks that are 8 feet or less above the ground. Support posts may also be made from 3 or 4 inch diameter Schedule 40 or thicker steel, or from masonry such as concrete blocks or bricks.

See Appendix II - the link to a free download
DCA6-12, for best practices.

Footings transfer the weight of the deck and anything
(or anyone) on the deck from the support posts to undisturbed solid ground. The area of the footing surface that touches the ground determines how much
weight the footing will carry without moving. Footings are often installed as an afterthought by pour-
ing a couple bags of concrete into a hole. While this
method may work in a few cases, footings should be
properly designed and installed.

How should support posts be installed?

The deck should be fastened to the support posts
and the support posts should be fastened to the footings. Proper fastening is necessary to keep the support posts from moving out from under the deck and
causing a catastrophic deck collapse.

Figure 16 shows the recommended methods for fastening support posts to the deck.

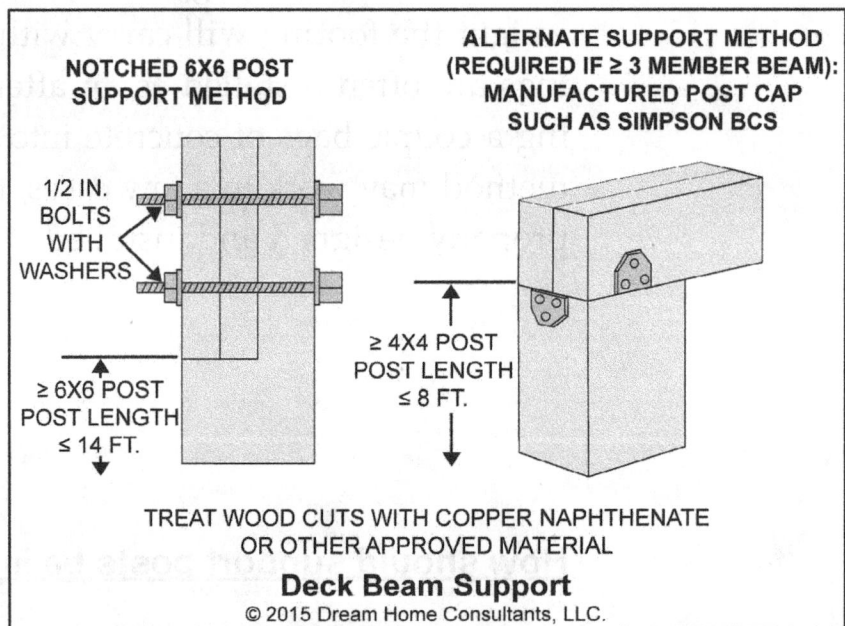

Figure 16

Figure 17 shows the recommended methods for fastening support posts to the footings. A post base on top of the footing is preferred because lumber (even treated lumber) embedded in concrete can rot over time. Rotting is especially likely if the cut end is embedded in concrete.

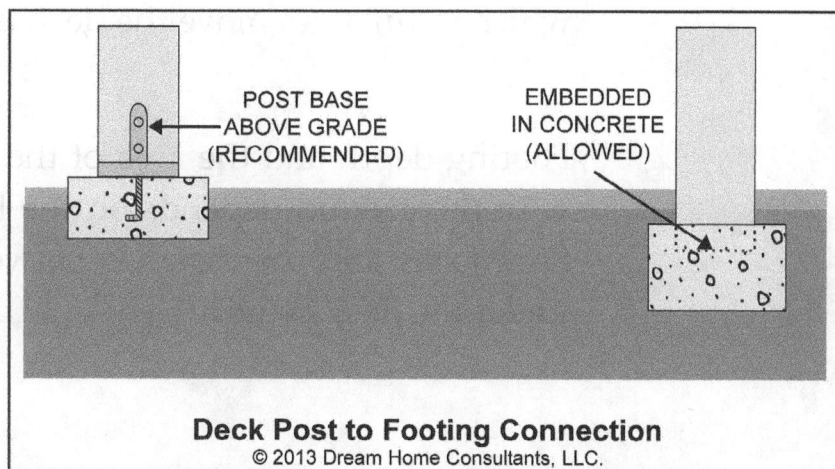

POST BASE
ABOVE GRADE
(RECOMMENDED)

EMBEDDED
IN CONCRETE
(ALLOWED)

Deck Post to Footing Connection
© 2013 Dream Home Consultants, LLC.

Figure 17

How should deck footings be installed?

Concrete footings should be installed on undisturbed or well-compacted soil using at least 2,500 psi rated concrete. The bottom of the footing should be below the local frost depth. Your building department can tell you the local frost line depth. These requirements help keep the footings from moving up or down which in turn can move the deck up or down.

Footing depth and the area of the footing in contact with the ground depends on the length of the deck floor joists and the distance between support posts under the deck beam.

Figure 18 shows some typical deck footing dimensions. The bottom of deck footings that are closer than 5 feet to the house foundation should be at the same level as the house footings. This helps keep the deck footings from putting stress on the house foundation that could cause foundation cracks and water intrusion.

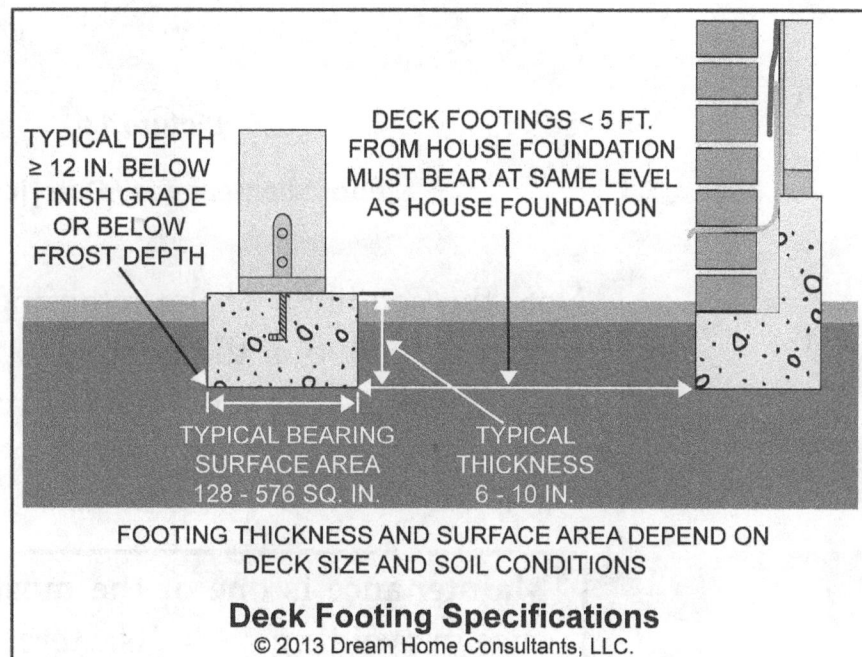

Figure 18

Picture 13

Poor Maintenance / Deterioration

Note the condition of the retaining wall. The posts shown at the top of the photo support a deck. A retaining wall may not be used to support a deck.

Maintenance is one of the most important issues in avoiding deck disasters.

Appendix I:

This table shows incidents **reported** since 2001.

A review of these news reports will show that a number of these incidents were attributed to lack of maintenance.

Appendix II:

Link to DCA6-12.

Appendix III:

What Makes a Qualified Contractor?

REMINDER:

Experts recommend that decks be inspected each year.

REMEMBER:

Codes and construction practices have changed as more and more incidents are reported and more injuries/fatalities occur.

Appendix I

Major Deck and Balcony Failures in the News 2001- AUG 2015

NOTE: The data reported were not collected as part of a formal study and reflect only a sample of injuries and fatalities that were widely publicized by media sources An analysis prepared for The Associated Press by the Consumer Product Safety Commission estimated that some 4,600 emergency room visits were associated with deck collapses, and another 1,900 with porch failures.   http://www.usnews.com/news/us/articles/2015/06/18/review-shows-deaths-seldom-occur-in-balcony-collapses

The table, Major Deck and Balcony Failures in the News 2001 – AUG 2015, was compiled by Frank Woeste and updated by Bruce A. Barker.

Grand Rapids MI	AUG 2015	1 injured
Emerald Isle NC	AUG 2015	9 injured
Brome Lake CA	AUG 2015	0 injuries
Columbia MD	JUL 2015	5 injured
Omaha NE	JUL 2015	2 injured

Rockland CO NY	JUL 2015	2 injured
Greely CO	JUL 2015	7 injured
New Bedford MA	JUL 2015	3 injured
Folsom CA	JUL 2015	1 fatality
Lehi UTAH	JUL 2015	4 injured
Emerald Isle NC	JUL 2015	24 injured
Berkeley CA	JUN 2015	7 injured, 6 fatalities
Yarmouth NS	JUN 2015	12 injured
Cole Harbour NS	JUN 2015	1 injured
Pittsburgh PA	JUN 2015	4 injured
Sitka AK	JUN 2015	2 injured
Evanston IL	MAY 2015	4 injured
Noblesville IN	May 2015	2 injured
Lithonia GA	MAY 2015	9 injured

* = actual number not reported

Cedarville OH	APR 2015	8 injured
Portland ME	APR 2015	1 fatality
Knoxville TN	APR 2015	1 injured
Beverly MA	APR 2015	1 injured
Higham MA	FEB 2015	* injured
San Francisco CA	JAN 2015	3 injured
Greenville SC	NOV 2014	22 injured
Halifax NS	SEP 2014	6 injured
Oakland CA	SEP 2014	9 injured
Towson MD	SEP 2014	7 injured
Ellenwood GA	SEP 2014	6 injured
Philadelphia PA	AUG 2014	1 injured
Atlanta GA	AUG 2014	5 injured
Valley NE	JUL 2014	2 injured

* = actual number not reported

Folsom CA	JUL 2014	0 injured
Penn Forest Twp PA	JUL 2014	6 injured
Ponte Vedra Beach FL	JUN 2014	4 injured
Staton Island NY	JUN 2014	1 injured
Pawleys Island SC	JUN 2014	13 injured
Stone Mountain GA	MAY 2014	13 injured
Stone Harbor NY	APR 2014	3 injured
Lynchburg VA	JAN 2014	1 injured, 1 fatality
New Albany IN	DEC 2013	* injured
Concord TWP DE	SEP 2013	7 injured
Dartmouth NS	SEP 2013	15 injured
Ocean Isle Beach NC	JUL 2013	21 injured
Miami FL	JUN 2013	33 injured
Long Beach NY	JUN 2013	5 injured

* = actual number not reported

Wildwood IL	MAY 2013	3 injured
Montgomery AL	MAY 2013	* injured
Gulf Shores AL	MAR 2013	7 injured
Montgomery AL	DEC 2012	2 injured
Powder Springs GA	SEP 2012	1 injured
Louisville, KY	JUL 2012	4 injured
Austin TX	JUL 2012	10 injured
Littleton CO	JUL 2012	4 injured
Atlanta GA	MAY 2012	7 injured
Ashland NH	MAY 2012	* injured
Churubusco IN	MAY 2012	* injured
Melrose MA	OCT 2011	1 fatality
Charlottesville VA	SEP 2011	2 injured
Trappe PA	SEP 2011	3 injured

* = actual number not reported

Castleton VT	SEP 2011	* injured
Golden CO	AUG 2011	12 injured
Philadelphia PA	SEP 2010	7 injured
Austin TX	AUG 2010	23 injured
Holden Beach NC	JUN 2010	7 injured
Lexington VA	MAY 2010	22 injured
Ocean Isle Beach NC	JUL 2009	21 injured
Wildwood MO	JUN 2009	9 injured
Cary IL	MAY 2009	2 injured
Richmond VA	NOV 2008	20 injured
Vancouver BC	OCT 2008	3 injured
Ottawa Ontario	JUN 2008	6 injured
Narragansett ME	JAN 2008	10 injured
Wildwood NJ	SEP 2007	* injured
Warwick RI	JUN 2007	5 injured

* = actual number not reported

Ship Bottom NJ	JUL 2007	7 injured
Vancouver BC	JUL 2007	2 injured
Oxford CT	JUL 2007	4 injured
Cape May NJ	JUL 2007	9 injured
Fall River KS	MAY 2007	* injured 1 fatality
Norman IL	MAY 2007	6 injured
Brooklyn MD	MAR 2007	4 injured
Smithtown NY	MAR 2007	7 injured
Melville NY	JAN 2007	3 injured
Lawrenceville GA	SEP 2006	4 injured
Concord MA	SEP 2006	6 injured
Arlington PA	AUG 2006	3 injured
Westerly RI	AUG 2006	9 injured
Fitchburg MA	AUG 2006	1 injured

* = actual number not reported

Pt. Pleas. Beach NJ	JUL 2006	6 injured
Needham MA	JUL 2006	2 injured
Howells NY	JUL 2006	15 injured
Covington KY	JUL 2006	1 injured
Upper Marlboro MD	JUN 2006	5 injured
Patterson NY	JUN 2006	1 injured
Kripplebush NY	JUN 2006	13 injured
Chesterfield VA	JUN 2006	4 injured
McGaheysville VA	JUN 2006	3 injured
Fitchburg MA	JUN 2006	1 injured
Philadelphia PA	JUN 2006	7 injured
Marietta GA	MAY 2006	3 injured
Kitchener ON	MAY 2006	2 injured
Chattanooga TN	MAY 2006	2 injured
Annapolis MD	JAN 2006	5 injured

* = actual number not reported

Chicago IL	DEC 2005	2 injured
Loveland OH	OCT 2005	13 injured
Virginia Beach VA	OCT 2005	33 injured
Seneca SC	SEP 2005	7 injured
Elm Grove WI	SEP 2005	9 injured
Minneapolis MN	SEP 2005	3 injured
Arlington Heights IL	AUG 2005	6 injured
Portland OR	AUG 2005	10 injured
Sherwood AR	AUG 2005	12 injured
Troy IL	JUL 2005	7 injured
Fort Kent ME	JUL 2005	5 injured
San Francisco CA	JUN 2005	3 injured
Chicago IL	JUN 2005	1 injured
Lincoln Park IL	JUN 2005	2 injured
Chicago IL	JUN 2005	1 fatality

* = actual number not reported   © 2015 Dream Home Consultants, LLC.

Allentown PA	JUN 2005	2 injured
Charlottesville VA	APR 2005	1 injured
Napa CA	APR 2005	11 injured
Durham NC	MAR 2005	3 injured
Columbus OH	NOV 2004	1 fatality
Pierce County WA	OCT 2004	7 injured, 1 fatality
Wilmington NC	OCT 2004	8 injured
Milford CT	SEP 2004	8 injured
St. Louis MO	AUG 2004	2 injured
Polson MT	JUL 2004	80 injured
Elyra OH	JUN 2004	6 injured
Victoria BC	MAY 2004	10 injured
Highlands NJ	FEB 2004	7 injured
Charlottesville VA	DEC 2003	1 injured, 1 fatality

* = actual number not reported

Chilmark MA	AUG 2003	10 injured
Queens NY	AUG 2003	3 injured, 1 fatality
Chula Vista AL	JUN 2003	23 injured
Chicago IL	JUN 2003	57 injured, 13 fatalities
Huntington WV	MAY 2003	17 injured
Exton PA	SEP 2002	11 injured
Egg Harbor NJ	JUL 2002	4 injured
Point Pleasant NJ	JUL 2002	33 injured
San Francisco CA	NOV 2001	1 injured
Sea Isle City NJ	AUG 2001	11 injured
Buffalo Grove IL	JUN 2001	3 injured
Quincy MA	MAY 2001	5 injured
Ossining NY	JUN 2001	19 injured
Parkland WA	FEB 2001	5 injured, 1 fatality

* = actual number not reported

Appendix II

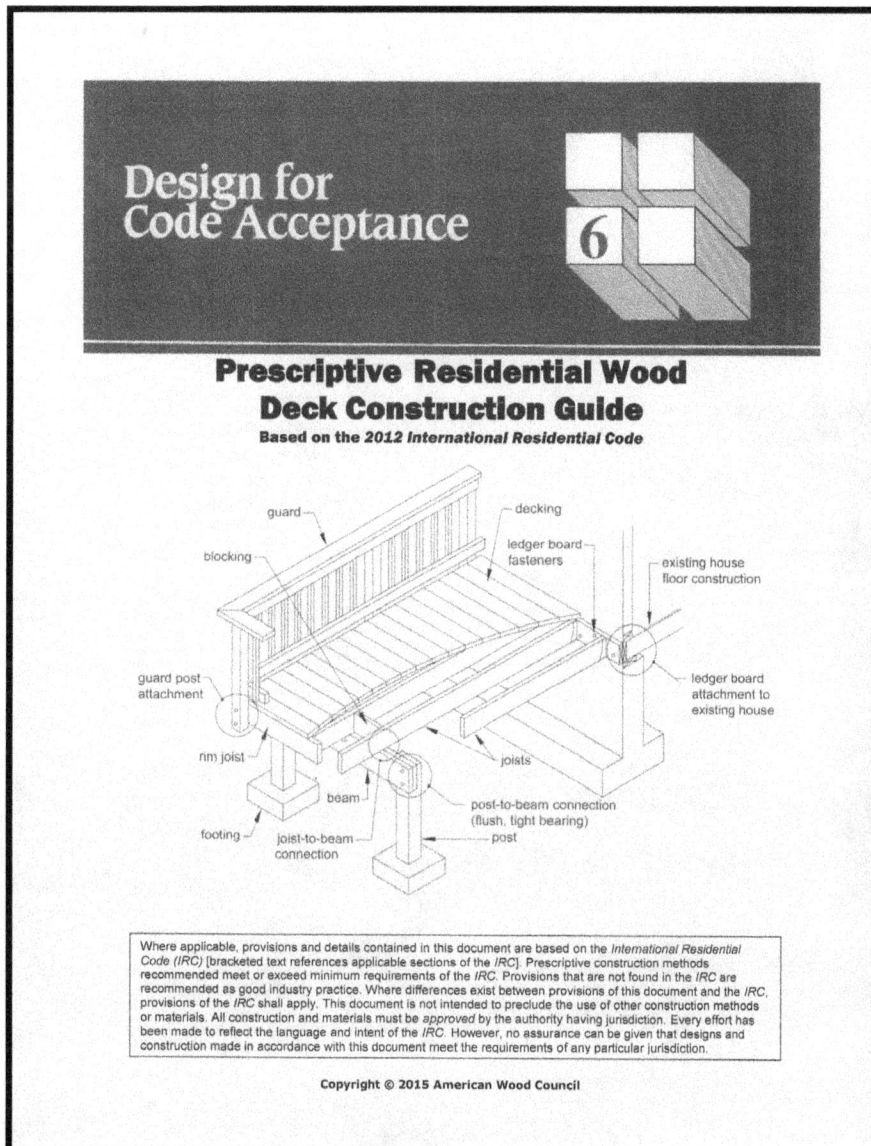

Prescriptive Residential Wood Deck Construction Guide
Based on the 2012 International Residential Code

http://www.awc.org/pdf/codes-standards/publications/dca/awc-dca62012-deckguide-1405.pdf

http://www.awc.org/pdf/codes-standards/publications/dca/awc-dca62012-deckguide-spanish-1507.pdf

Appendix III

Good contractors are a little like hen's teeth. Often it seems as though there are not any. Good contractors are out there, the problem is finding them. Nothing you do guarantees that the contractor you hire will be a good one, and even good ones can do bad jobs. The following are some steps that will help improve the chance of finding, and successfully working with, a good contactor. For the sake of this discussion, we will assume that good contractors are also qualified contractors. This is usually true.

Check Out the Contractor

The first step in finding a good contractor is verifying the contractor's essential credentials.

1. Verify the contractor's license. Most states require contractors to be licensed and most states have websites where you can verify the contractor's license. You can often find information about complaints filed against the contractor at this site. Only use licensed contractors. A license is not a guarantee of a good contractor, but lack of a license is often a sign of a bad contractor.

2. Obtain the contractor's certificate of insurance. A good contractor will be happy to provide a certificate from his/her insurance company, thus making it easy for the homeowner to verify with the insurance company. (Because from time to time, the information provided is outdated or perhaps does not exist, the homeowner should verify the contractor's insurance coverage.)

The ideal contractor has general liability and workman's compensation insurance. General liability protects you in case the contractor damages something. Workman's compensation protects you in case a worker is injured while on your property. Yes, you could be sued by a worker injured on your property. Workman's compensation insurance is very expensive and not all contractors carry it. Not having general liability and workman's compensation isn't a deal breaker, but it is a risk consideration. Also, check what coverage your homeowner's insurance policy might provide if a worker is injured while on your property.

3. Check references, but not only those the contractor gives you. Check sites like Yelp and enter the contractor into a search engine like Google.

Define the Scope of Work

A written scope of work definition is one of the best ways to avoid misunderstandings and the disasters that often follow. Be as precise as possible, but make allowances for the size of the job. A simple scope definition is appropriate for a simple job.

1. Identify products and materials to be used. For example, products and materials used to build a

deck would include the types and sizes of lumber and other structural materials, the types of fasteners and other hardware such as joist hangers, and the types of flashing.

2. Identify the important work tasks to be performed. For example, a work task to build a deck would include producing a plan showing all details necessary to obtain a building permit, obtaining the building permit, removing and disposing of any existing deck, and removing and disposing of construction debris.

3. Specify that the contractor will perform all work in strict compliance with all building codes and will follow the manufacturer's instructions. This should occur regardless, but it helps to have it in writing.

4. Specify that the work will be performed under a building permit, if required in your jurisdiction. This should occur regardless, but it helps to have it in writing. **Be very concerned if a contractor does not want to perform the work under a building permit.**

Define the Payment Schedule

The complexity of the payment schedule depends on the complexity of the work. Small projects may have two or three payments. Large projects may have several progress payments. Typical payments include some amount upon signing of an agreement, progress payments, and the final payment.

1. Pay not more than ten percent of the total contract price upon signing the agreement for the job. If materials need to be special-ordered, this number may increase as reasonably necessary to pay for these materials. Rarely should the initial payment exceed twenty-five percent. (If the contractor asks for a large percentage, this may be a bad sign. Also, if the contractor asks for an advance, especially long before the start date, this may be a bad sign.)

2. Tie progress payments to completion of specific work tasks. For example, removing and disposing of an existing deck might be worth twenty percent.

3. Make a final payment of ten to twenty-five percent when all work is completed according to the written agreement, including passing the building department inspection.

Define a Change Order Procedure (and Stick to It)

Expect the unexpected during home improvement projects, especially large deck building projects. Changes to the scope of work should only be made with a written agreement that describes the scope change and the price change. You and the contractor should sign the change order agreement. It is tempting to ignore change orders during the crunch of a project deadline, but both you and the contractor do so at your peril. Lack of written change orders causes more disagreements between contractors and customers than almost any other problem.

The Bottom Line

It is said that if you do not know where you are going, any road will take you there. Proper planning and a good written agreement will help you and your contractor arrive at your destination.

References

American Wood Council 2013. *Prescriptive Residential Wood Deck Construction Guide Based on the 2012 International Residential Code* (DCA6-12 2013 Edition).

Anderson, Cheryl, Dr. Frank Woeste, and Dr. Joseph Loferski, *Manual for the Inspection of Residential Wood Decks and Balconies.* Madison WI: Forest Products Society in cooperation with the International Code Council, 2003.

Barker, Bruce A. *Everybody's Building Code.* Cary, NC: Dream Home Consultants, LLC, 2015.

Bender, Don. Weyerhaeuser Professor, Washington State University. Personal communication. April 2015.

Bouldin, John. Virginia Tech University. Personal communication. March 2015.

International Code Council. *2015 International Residential Code for One- and Two- family Dwellings.* Country Club Hills, IL: International Code Council, Inc., 2014.

Loferski, Joseph, and Frank Woeste, P.E, with Dustin Albright and Ricky Caudill. "Strong Rail-Post Connections for Wooden Decks," *Journal of Light Construction,* February 2005.

West, Anne W. "Deck Inspections: A matter of life and death," reprinted in the *ASHI Reporter,* July 2007.

Woeste, Frank 2008. "Coastal Resources: Safe and Durable Coastal Decks," *Journal of Light Construction,* March 2008.

Woeste, Frank. Virginia Tech University. Personal communication. April 2015.

Index

About the Author

Bruce A. Barker is President of Dream Home Consultants, LLC., a building inspection and consulting firm. He has built or inspected more than 3,000 homes during his 28 years in the construction and building inspection industries. Bruce is certified by the International Code Council as a Residential Combination Inspector. He is a licensed contractor in North Carolina, Arizona, and Florida, and a licensed home inspector in North Carolina and Arizona.

Bruce is on the Board of the American Society of Home Inspectors (ASHI) and an ACI (ASHI Certified Inspector). He began his three year term on ASHI's Board after serving six years as Chairman of the Standards of Practice Committee. He also serves as a subject matter expert for the National Home Inspector Examination (NHIE).

Other Books by Bruce A. Barker

Black & Decker Codes for Homeowners

Black & Decker Codes for Homeowners, Second Edition

Black & Decker Codes for Homeowners, Updated Third Edition

Everybody's Building Code, 2003

Everybody's Building Code, 2009

Everybody's Building Code, 2012

Everybody's Building Code, 2015

NHIE Home Inspection Manual, 2015

* 9 7 8 0 9 8 4 8 1 6 0 3 3 *